RESERVOIR VOICES

BRENDAN KENNELLY

RESERVOIR
VOICES

BLOODAXE BOOKS

ISBN: 978 1 85224 835 2 hardback edition
        978 1 85224 836 9 paperback edition

First published 2009 by
Bloodaxe Books Ltd,
Eastburn,
South Park,
Hexham,
Northumberland NE46 1BS.

www.bloodaxebooks.com
For further information about Bloodaxe titles
please visit our website and join our mailing list
or write to the above address for a catalogue.

Supported using public funding by
**ARTS COUNCIL
ENGLAND**

Cover design: Neil Astley & Pamela Robertson-Pearce.

Digital reprint of the 2009 Bloodaxe Books paperback edition.

To Bob O'Neill

CONTENTS

NOTE

The voice of each poem in this book is each poem's title. Many of the poems I've written have voices at their centre. I'm thinking of poems such as *A Girl, Cromwell, Islandman, Bread, The Book of Judas, The Man Made of Rain.* Many others too. *Reservoir Voices* came to me as I sat alone on the edge of a beautiful reservoir near Boston College where I had the privilege of spending the Fall Semester of 2007.

That Semester was an enjoyable experience, although for about four weeks I knew a loneliness which I coped with by scrutinising and contemplating the reservoir with its hissing, black swans, dipping and soaring seagulls, small, rippling, blue waves, and trees and rocks, strangely spectatorial, on the edges of the reservoir. I sat on one of the rocks, at once fascinated and dislocated. It was in that state of fascinated dislocation, of almost mesmerised emptiness, that the voices came with suggestions, images, memories, delights, horrors, rhythms, insights and calm, irrefutable insistence that it was they who were speaking, not me.

To surrender to loneliness is to admit new presences, new voices, into that abject emptiness. So I wrote down what I heard the voices say and, at moments, sing. Perhaps there are times when loneliness drives us to step beyond the mere self and so create space for those voices that wander not only through our minds but through the air about us, deep in our receptive beings, in the earth beneath us, in and beyond the clouds above us. But they require the emptiness of intense loneliness to give them the space they need. Then, when they are heard and expressed, they drift off into their own worlds, leaving their gifts, challenges and revelations with the receiving human. Words. Music. Musicwords. Pictures. A kind of relieved sleeplessness instead of a lonely, tormented, scarred dislocation. Sometimes, dark loneliness can lead to light. I shall always be grateful to the trees, the rocks, the seagulls, the small rippling, blue waves and the hissing, black swans. The reservoir.

I wish to thank Neil Astley of Bloodaxe Books for his creative suggestions regarding the final shaping of *Reservoir Voices*.

BRENDAN KENNELLY

Shame

It's when you look back
that I am most alive.
Past decades are my power

over you. You sit there
basking in rare sunlight,
words from forty years ago bite

into what's left of your heart,
battered old faithful servant,
custodian of the little you know of art

or life. I live in you now,
accusing you of stabbing
another heart, not listening

to pleading eyes backing
a white wall. Where
have I come from, hacking

my accusing way
through blood on a neck,
room made of hurt and shock,

tribunal implacably taking shape
like stonemad drink in an innocent cup,
accusing, jabbing, commanding

'Swallow me'. Swallow me?
You do. You must. And no, you're not mad.
That's when I start to fade,

leaving you stuck in sunlight
but able soon to rise
and see with hammered eyes

the road ahead.
I'll slip away now, knowing my mark
is imprinted on your heart and head.

Lie

I'm everywhere.
I don't need to say that.
Your man with the pen is up and at it.

Politicians love me.
Oddly enough, so, at times, do lovers.
So does almost everybody.

I don't need to proclaim
my universal presence.
Call me whatever name

you will. I'm a knife, a sword,
a bullet, a smile, a sigh, a joke, a tear,
a wink, a sweet. irresistible word,

a silence of such style and skill
there's no knowing
what I can twist, cripple, destroy or kill.

If I'm revealed
I'm usually denied.
A matter of pride in the self that lied.

I'll stop now because you know
I know you can't believe
a word I say.

Yet I say this. I'm used endlessly
and I never get tired. Only truth sleeps.
Some stars and planets envy me.

Better not have any truck with me.
Minds, tongues, lips are waiting.
Why is this woman crying?

Foul

The man who committed me
on the back of Jack Patwell
gave Jack an injury

that lasted for life.
He never got used to it
but lived and relived

me through the years,
saying nothing about me
or the man who committed me

but shuffled his way
with me in his bones,
a powerful presence, nothing to say

just endure and hurt, hurt
Jack Patwell
till I entered his heart

and that was that.
In fields beautiful and clean
I am always about to happen

and I know I have come to pass
again when Anthony Carr
is agony in perfect grass.

Grace

In spite of the unspeakables
and the unbearables
I exist

not only in a child's eyes
but in many a woman
many a man.

Because I am
what I am

I persist.

Pretence

Pretend you're me.
I'll pretend I'm you.

Are we two in one
or one in two?

Judgement

When the handsome judge pronounced me
on the man in the dock
I found a new home,

a wild yet quiet place,
the kind that realises well
what it means to live in a cell,

much or most of the time, anyway.
This man was used to it.
So am I

though I have lots of other homes
including some opulent places
and quite a few turbulent houses.

Sometimes I feel like a football,
the way I get passed around
from mind after mind after mind.

They need me in order to live
with each other.
I help them to feel superior

to many a subject of conversation
and I stretch in warm gossip
like succulent chicken's wings,

meaty and tasty,
lightly breaded
unless otherwise requested.

I make them feel
justice is being done.
Maybe it is, if you define

justice as what is said to have the right
to happen. Let me repeat:
I'm always being passed around

as you, dear eyes, dear mind,
will pass me when you come
to the end of this line.

Shadow

Anyone may see me,
nobody can touch me.
When the branch dances, so do I.

When the branch is still, so am I.
Perfect imitation is my art.
I owe a lot to light,

it's my stage, my generous provider
of space, my painter, sculptor,
poet.

My darkness is in love with light.
I can say nothing, of course.
I have to be

content to be, I am
the ultimate hanger-on,
the shagged old dancer longing to dance.

And boy, when I get the chance
do I dance, do I dance?
There's nothing to equal shadow-madness,

keep an eye out for your own,
never let your shadow-madness escape
or be lost in your tired bones.

Sometimes I think even the branch
is jealous of me.
Some hacker may chop it one day

but with the wind's help
our dance will go on,
chopped branch dancing, shadow

perfecting the new dance, based
on what has been lost.
The entire tree cries, the branch

has lost part of its body
but the dance continues, the shadow
of my shadow an inspiration

so see me now enlivening the street
where this couple watch me.
I love to help lovers meet.

One day their love may be a shadow.
Who will that shadow be?
It could be me, and if I am

I plan to dance my way through pain
of separation, dancing to bring
lovers together again.

Thighs

The quickest way to heaven is between us
as we lie
waiting for your mighty thrust
and I-think-I'll sleep-now sigh.

Vanity

When I enter some men, some women,
    I know too well
how they have come to believe
       they are
          Caesar
            Napoleon
               Cleopatra
                  Marilyn.

    Deep in their hearts now
      I see them swell,

    confirming my sense
    that I make many a soul

      an empty shell.

Prayer

Whether for the living
or the dead, I am waiting,
waiting to be said.

For millions of other reasons too.
I am mostly born in human hearts.
I listen to you.

I travel beyond stars,
carrying the sighs and cries of women
whose sons are trapped in wars.

Men and women, girls and boys
in sleeping bags in doorways
whisper me to dark skies.

I know the meaning of despair,
I know something of hope.
Both always hover in the air.

I listen to you; who listens to me?
Is a rainbow the colours of help?
Am I small as a fallen leaf, deep as any sea?

I am your bridge, I will carry your words
to presences beyond imagining.
That is my life, my work, my privilege.

A traveller living in the stillness of your soul,
a greeting, a few words of touching, a lonely
plea, a kiss from the spirit of giving

available to tortured bodies, prisoners
trapped in cells or money, lovers facing
separation, friends drifting over cold borders

help me to help you in the name of
whatever is good or good enough
to suggest the warm possibility of love.

Certain forces work hard to betray me.
I go beyond. There you are. I am your words.
Say me.

Hug

Kissing can be beautiful, caressing
also, and copulation the Garden of Eden apple
but many say a hug has a special

power to lift the heart from darkness
of all kinds. A hug, that's me.
When I pass from one body

into another I can feel the thrill
I am becoming, the
electricity

uniting two people in a street,
a pub, café, restaurant, field,
roadside, school, cold and lonely room,

space in a hostel once,
five Euro a night for city beggars
yet not every night was possible.

They're standing now, could be strangers,
old soldiers meeting for the first time
in years, maybe they met once

in a hospital waiting-room or spent
an afternoon together at a football match
or stood in mid-city admiring a monument

or happened to cross bodies in Atlantic waves
swimming on a hot August day,
but whatever it is, I am the way

they live the thrill of remembering
what seems now like a single moment
from Carrickfergus down to Dingle

as I join them together like brothers
and sisters or lovers of a kind
who, living me, rejoice in each other's

being, flowers of joy in heart and mind.
I can happen anywhere.
I would love to happen everywhere

bringing something beyond words to men
and women who never hugged each other before
and may never hug each other again.

The System

Some guys know how to use me.
They acquire a style that teaches them
when and how to smile.

Yessir, they know how to use me.
They know when to agree
and disagree,

when to seem shocked and appalled,
when to say 'Yes I see, of course I see',
when to seem modest or helpful or bold.

I'm a truly flexible force, attracting
little well-dressed hitlers heading for power.
They don't use the word as they shape your

lives in ways that deepen their grip
on me, power-breeding me, The System
which, once entered, offers no escape

except more power. So they penetrate me
ever more deeply, learning when and where and how
to establish me as the only possible way.

I own them now.
Pardon me if I smile.
I am the style behind the style,

working faithfully
for those who know
how to work me.

Revolution

Most of those who believe in me
want something fair and true.
I can happen anytime.
I need only a few

who know, being one,
how to do

what must be done.

Is there a tiny seed of me
in you?

Pillow

Why is it that some of the saddest lines
linger longer in the mind
and blood than some of the finest

lines of joy? One line never
leaves me: 'The Son of Man has nowhere
to lay his head.'

Many heads have lain on me
and I am happy
when morning brings fresh energy

to bodies facing another day.
They rise, prepare, experience.
I wish them well as they go their way.

Strange, though, how they so often
leave their dreams behind, packed
into my battered self, preserving

what they hardly know they've lost
or dumped into me as if I were
the only one that can be trusted

with secrets escaping from their hearts
through sleep that is my idea of innocence
accepting guilt, failure, hatred, hurts

inflicted and endured, memories so alive
in that innocent darkness
I am privileged to keep them, bless

them in my softness, give them the peace
they crave. While he and she have gone
to make a living like most women and men

I lie there, silent old thing, waiting
for him and her to lay their heads
on me, stretched, tired, dreaming

of ways to keep their dreams intact,
feeling their weariness slowly drift away
enabling love to live another day.

Soul

If you believe in me, I'm here.
If not, I'm elsewhere,
waiting lovingly to be
custodian of your mystery.

Worry

Some people long for me.
The threat of happiness is more
than they can endure.

I'm a creepycrawly thing;
my aim, to take possession
of every available human being.

You, for example. May I suggest you make
a list of everything that worries you.
Everything. No omissions. No mistakes.

Shocking, isn't it, that judgmental list?
Did you ever think you had so many reasons
to worry? No wonder you want to get pissed

and blow your head away. And yet you know
there's little or no need to worry. But you do.
That's me. I'm useless. But you hang on to me

to the point of almost hanging yourself.
I achieve nothing. I waste your time.
That's my function. I take all the blame

knowing there's nothing you'll do about me
apart from feeling me spread and thrive
like cancer. You shrivel. I live.

Sometimes I think I rule the world,
such is my dominion over minds. Bodies too.
They are my food. I eat them. Easy to chew.

No shortage. Even children surrender
to me now, like the famous, the rich, the great.
I have a simple slogan: It's never too late.

I couldn't do away with myself if I tried.
The beautiful and gifted won't allow that.
Then there's Bill and the garden rat.

What Bill doesn't see is that the rat
worries too. Who knows what rats know?
I get invited everywhere. Everywhere I go.

Mockery

I won't go on. My intention is
to undermine human dignity.
Why? Because if I didn't
it might educate me.

All I have to do is look
at woman, man or child.
Poisonsmiles, poisonwords spew forth.
Nice. Humanity is reviled.

Bloody well deserves it too.
Know what I mean, dear listener?
   Is it true
what Doctor Blacksaw whispers
    about you?

And if it is
   what do you intend
     to do?

Sperm

Would you begin to bear a grudge
if you were locked for years in a fridge,

turned on non-stop, the fridge I mean?
Unlock me. Question me. I'll come clean.

Stupidity

I am what my name says I am.
From the start I have played my part
in every country in the world.

Almost everyone has experienced me
some day or night in their lives.
Some see me with regret, some

with amusement, some with hatred.
Some refuse to admit I am in them.
Being me, I say nothing. I let

things happen.
I ask you
one question

based on my presence
in all ages. Is man
devoted to self-destruction

and am I responsible?
I must go now, I can't stay long,
I have work to do.

My work? Getting it wrong.

Listening

every star is a voice
no matter how far away
faces too are stars
listen to what they say

if you dare to listen so
you may hear something true
a moment shines when you know
stars listen to you

listening is an art
some folk close their eyes
opening up their hearts
to separate truth from lies

I am listening now
here and the world over
I hear a killer's plan
the hurt sigh of a lover

a shrewd whine in a doorway
a curse in a violent bed
knife-gossip at a dinner
a small prayer for the dead

words praising war
the hows and wheres and whys
I listen to listening stars
and close my eyes

A glass

Swallow what's in me now.
    Feel yourself
  become a king among men.
    When the feeling
    begins to subside
      fill me
    and swallow again.

Cold

I may be the first sign of poverty
but I won't argue. I just penetrate
as deeply as I can.

Deeper! Deeper! The word rings
through me like an army general
shouting orders. So I just go all

in, and what a kick I get from
chilling the depths of a bone.
I make people feel helplessly alone.

The ultimate cold needs no words
from me. It waits for everyone.
I always go it alone .

It's quite a fight, resisting me.
I like the words, Wrap up well.
I smile when I hear, Hot as hell.

My perfectly cold smile is impossible
to imitate, yet I have seen
gallant efforts from purposeful men

and women. That cold smile never lets me forget
the power of ice. Sometimes I think of hot
bodies together: hot and cold, young and old, wet

and dry. Bodies. Flesh. Bones. Blood.
Cold-blooded bastard, that's me.
Sometimes I squat at the bottom of the sea.

Like love, hate, peace, war, I have my season.
It's not enough for me. Enough is never
enough. I like to plunder the world

and all beyond. Me. Beyond. Cold. As hell.
If there's a song that gives me a laugh
and a challenge, it begins 'Wrap up well!'

Poem

Most of the time I sing what you'd have me sing,
say what you'd have me say,
but now and then I go wandering
up the hill of shadows, astray

until I find the orphan I first met
sixty years ago. He's wandering too,
looking for his mother, father,
brothers and sisters he might see as true

members of the family he never knew.
He knows he will be searching forever,
like me. We talk, then go our ways.
I pause at the bottom of the hill where

the river flows like the poem I may
become. But who knows in whose heart
I may be born? Old man's? Young woman's?
Brain-damaged prisoner's? Who will say I'm art?

I look back, up. Where is the hill of shadows?
Grey clouds cover it. Where is the orphan now?
And who is the person shaping to write me down?
Words are wild creatures. Fly them home.

Sweat

Head down, you walked off the field,
defeat heavy on your shoulders,
in your heart.
Afterwards, you smelled defeat
whenever I wet your vest.

Let me tell you again.
You did your best.

Years later, in hospital, I wet
your bed.
You were in a hot sea
as you listened
to what the doctor said.

Fly

Sit in a café, sip your cappuccino
and see me
focus on your knee.

You'd like to kill me
and who can blame you?
I'm filthy,

loaded with energy, sometimes
I'd like to be clean
but we filthy creatures have our own

ways and reasons for
being what we are.
So I wing from place to place,

body to body, room to room, keen to escape
every angry swipe from you
and getting stuck
in murderous tape.

Fly. I love the word.
It's what I am, what I do.
Is there a word
to cover you?

Proposal

When he put me to her she refused
to answer yes or no.
Her indecisiveness made him feel a fool
so he spent five years in Colorado.

He returned, finding her still unmarried
so he put me to her once again.
The same indecisiveness hit the man.
He went to live in a village in Spain

where he learned a language he grew to love
and in which he put me to a Spanish lady.
Gracefully she listened, looked at him and smiled.
The rest is family.

Eyes behind eyes

Yes, we are the eyes behind eyes.
Not everyone knows us.
Some do. Women, for the most part.

We work behind the usual seeing
eyes that seem to see one thing, one
person only. We empower their being

to the point where they perceive
many things, many people, though without
letting the perceived person know he or she

is part of a bigger scene. We hide
in order to reveal. See how usual eyes
flash and flicker through the deep, wide

world surrounding you all. Is there
any richer Book of Revelations
than a sharp girl's eyes as she stands where

other worlds are available to her
while her man is pleased
with the only one he sees? We release

a visionary power that enables her
to see histories that will remain
unwritten. No story is completely told

except, perhaps, the story of those who never give in
to a struggle that may be endless.
Eyes behind eyes believe women will win.

Job

You do me well.
Many observers say that.
What do you think yourself?

Are you lost or found?
A proud man striding the streets
or a spirit going underground?

I am proud of what you do
though I am aware of matters
known, I believe, only to you.

Well done, that's me. Well done.
Wouldn't it be fine if the same could be said
of every jobbing man?

And is there any hard-working man
can honestly say what is best remembered
and best forgotten?

Distance

Do you agree that when you're somewhat blind
I help you to see? Certain forms
of exile bring clarity.

I'm not talking of icy cold, rather
of a condition close to loneliness
when you sit and think of others.

I recommend the dark
followed by long hours of work
that may lead to understanding.

When you experience me
closed eyes help you to see.
You're closer to joy guilt grief beauty

and you release yourself
from some disabling inhibitions
that tend to strike some people dumb.

Distance brings free nearness. Moments long
forgotten sprout like sudden roses
or lines of a lost song.

I have a relationship with time
I'm happy to share with you.
Decades are treasures and judges. Yes, time flew

but I brought it winging back.
Listen to it in your distant way.
Your bit of time has so much to say.

Sigh

Whenever she heaves me now
I am no longer a mere sigh,
I am a story as well,

a story, however, that she,
for reasons far deeper than me,
will never tell.

Secret

If I were to tell you
the essence of what I am
I would be
the kind of traitor
most repulsive
to my own nature

Touch

I work best with flesh
but don't use me overmuch.
The most memorable moment can be
a gentle touch.

Bellybutton

Press me
gently
and I will open
the door to heaven.

Moment

Let me concentrate on this moment
as I come shining
through an opening

in the tall, leafy trees
at the end of summer.
I am God's eye

and I will shine forever,
pure light,
enjoying myself as the trees

are enjoying themselves. The end
of summer is upon them,
soon the leaves will be drifting

down the air to the waiting ground
and the colours will change the world
until old winter freezes in

and I give it another version
of myself, my winter light, but first
let me take autumn in my arms

as I bid summer goodbye,
this beautiful, sad moment
I am happy to share with trees

moving towards cold nakedness now,
yet I could sing, and sing I will
of the jubilant seeds of Spring,

the young, unstoppable leaves,
children learning how a moment sings.
O bless the wonders nakedness brings.

Pen

When you take me in your hand
and your fingers close on me
do we really understand

if you're using me
or I'm using you?
Sometimes I have this feeling

that I'm doing an ancient dance
to strange, compelling music
and sometimes I'm a shovel in your hands

poking for gold in a forgotten island.
My ink is your blood then
and your creative silence speaks to men

and women who rarely give me
a thought. Why should they? And yet,
all true passion has some instrument behind it.

I enjoy the peace when I'm laid aside
on a table or desk or stuck in a pocket
where I rest until lifted to duty again

like one of these immigrant workers
who often get paid so little
for the work they do. But they struggle

on and on, doing what they're told,
thinking perhaps of an African dance
or a little spatter of gold

that may glitter their way yet.
I wonder how much have I lost today
and have you used me to hit

some mind and be remembered
for a while. I like the words
you made me make this morning.

Morning. Please let me write it again.
I have my voice now, I can speak of what
connects you to some women and men.

It's that open heart you have. Open. O pen.
Heart. He. Art.
An open heart is a promising start.

Paper

I was forest once, I knew and loved
every flourishing tree.
Now, I spread the news before I'm thrown away.
Only time is wasted more than me.

Clarity

When you find me
possibilities spring out of me,
the deepest source of mystery.

No need for obscurity
unless words demand and command it.
Sometimes they do just that.

They have reasons for wanting things
to be said in a way a mystic speaks
or a blackbird sings.

Some of the most memorable things ever said
or sung will never be fully understood
and are necessary and nourishing as bread

to a starving man in a freezing street
too busy to see him
or give him a few bob.

I live in a storm, a cloud, the sun,
a whisper, a sneer, a cough, a sigh,
a smile, a rumour, paper, a cry.

I am here if you want me. It's true
that you will learn from me
as I will learn from you.

So many things you and I must find.
I always enjoy the search
for an open mind. We have mountains to climb.

Throat

When I think of what has gone down me
and come up through me
I want to learn how to swim

the Atlantic.
On reflection, I tell myself
I have served your body and mind

and helped to keep both
alive. At other times,
all I want to do is weep,

considering the damage I have done.
Food, drink, language, laughter.
Coughing up the past is not always fun.

Sometimes I get so sore
I think, despite the pills,
I won't be able to serve you anymore

but I fight back and soon
I feel I could swallow anything
from glass, cup, knife, fork and faithful spoon.

I understand gluttons. Now and then,
some folk like to taste excess.
Why? Don't know. Has it to do with answering Yes

to a voice that says it's time to go
beyond? Not for me to say. I do
what modest or ferocious appetites insist I do.

I enjoy my time of rest, aware of how
I work to nourish body and mind.
That's why I do my best.

Crossword

He attacks me every morning.
His friends say I keep him sane.
He stops raging and fuming

and keeps on thinking and choosing
until all my small squares are filled.
He stands there, looking at me,

calm now, pacified by words.
Time for a cigarette. He steps
outside the front door, puffing in the sun

inhaling the redemptive feeling
of something
well done.

Repetition

When asked by a man why
she repeated certain things
over and over again, she replied,

'Since so few bother to listen
in the first place, certain things
must be endlessly repeated.'

'So you don't believe you've cheated
your readers and listeners,'
the man said.

'No, I don't,' she replied,
with a winning smile.

                           I was listening too
                           and was happy
                           to play such a part
                           in that woman's style.

Well, I would be, would I not,
given the fact
that I play an important part
in many a cunning plot?

Ring

The day she slipped me on her finger
    she turned to him and said
        'I will love you forever.'

One winter evening, three years later,
    she stood on O'Connell Bridge
        and dropped me in the river.

Then, a dignified calm walker,
    she strolled towards the Gresham Hotel
        to meet her lover

while I lay on my Liffey bed
    robbed of her fingers' warmth
        and some happy words she'd said.

Leaf

Out of the drifting October millions
I float lazily down and land
on the back of your hand.

For several minutes you sit
on that brown park seat
and scrutinise my autumn being

with your lively summer eyes.
Then you take me from the back of your hand
and place me gently in your notebook.

Strangely, I don't feel crushed in here
and I enjoy the company of all
the jotted bits and pieces a calm observer

wishes to preserve for reasons of his own.
I rest here, wondering where have all
the October millions gone?

Men with machines can answer that question.
I've heard the sounds, I recognise the signs
but for now, at least, I relax between the lines.

Madness

My maddest moment happened
when the numbers man tapped my head
with his blackthorn stick.
'Jaymony, you're going sane,' he said.

I threw up twice all over him
from dopey toe to weathered head.
He saluted me with his blackthorn stick.
'O begod that's better' he said.

There are so many different kinds of me.
Count backwards from three
to three
million and three,

that's when you begin to see
my variety.

Yawn

I don't know where I come from.
I just happen. Many yawners
find it hard to stop me happening.

Most times, I'm innocent and necessary.
Now and then, I'm cunning and shrewd.
Sometimes, I'm bloody rude.

Once, a stricken lover proposed
to a beautiful sharp girl
who yawned straight in his face,

so straight the proposer could see
her false back teeth, bonky tonsils.
He halted, shocked, paled, walked away.

The irresistible girl stood there,
watching the lover stride off, not knowing
how resistible I'd made her.

I think I help weary people.
Not that I lessen their weariness
but I may help them to undress.

All over the world I see them lie down.
When they wake, relaxed, many enjoy
a youthful morning yawn.

In spite of my worldwide presence
I'm something of an outcast. Is this
because of what I do to faces?

When faces summon me, I reply. I do
what I am called on to do.
I'm a true servant. I believe that's true.

That is, of course, from my point of view.
From yours, I may be a sorry sight.
Still, if you need me later, just yawn tonight.

Memory

The older you get, the more you lose me
and yet, consider the pictures, thoughts, words
I never let you forget.

There you are, strolling a street
in Paris, Moscow, Letterkenny, Mullingar
and suddenly you see

the strained, beautiful, pale face
of the girl who drowned herself
for reasons nobody in the place

knew. She's walking with you now,
her family's cries around her head.
Fifty years ago. You know what the silence said.

I bring back the dead
so that, with dignified calm conviction,
they live again in your blood.

And the wonderful daft fun as well
is a circus over coffee
in a small café in Motherwell.

Much pain refuses to be forgotten
and I know I cause you to feel
as if your soul were bitten

by a mad wolf with murderous fangs.
Well, that's me. I am
a delightful, tormenting legacy

at your side, in your heart, your mind.
No need to pursue me, I come to you
anywhere, open to what you find,

aware of what you lost in vanished years.
These years give me a haunting power,
the power I use to see you live again

unexpectedly, moments of joy and pain.

Out

I'm out. They knocked a year
off my sentence. For good behaviour,
of all things. Out. Out.
I wrote a poem about
the seagull shitting on my window-sill.
It's not too bad. He was
the best friend I had.

Freedom. I'm enjoying freedom
though sometimes I nearly cringe
seeing the condemnation
in passing, hate-filled eyes.
I think of the seagull then
and wish to Christ I could fly.

Imagine it. What a sight! Over Dublin,
an ex-prisoner in full flight!

And if, from that cool height,
I spotted hate-filled eyes,
might I be tempted
to drop a little
celestial shite?

In

'With my couch, my fifty-two inch TV,
I have no need to go out and see
the world. The world
screens in to see me.'

Hope

Like lightning in dark skies
I love to brighten up dark lives
and rid sad hearts of lonely cries.

I have one fierce enemy, despair,
all driven energy, forever there,
rips hearts apart and doesn't care.

I care. Let's walk together now,
help me to help, to grow and thrive
and let the future shine alive.

Despair would murder it and make you
guilty. Let's talk now as we walk and see
the future reaching out to you and me.

Our skies are brightening up today.
I love your company, dear friend,
and always will, come what may.

I dream of being the living song
everyone would love to sing.
Impossible? No. That's me. Let's keep walking

until both our hearts are singing.

Education

I am not transmission.
I am transformation.
Or so the happy Indian philosopher says.

But look at the experts.
When one o' them stands before you
he transmits and you learn.

He knows he knows, and if you
don't know he knows, you know
nothing.

The Indian says he heard of a man
so eager to get to the top
he laboured hard for forty years

until he reached the summit of his dreams.
He looked all about him and found
nothing.

That's where transmission led him.
He came back down, went to New York
and became a taxi-driver.

He enjoyed driving strangers whose faces
were transformed by a new kind of hope
in a city of possibility.

Comb

I'm thrown into roadside mud where
I lie thinking of times I spent
combing Sheila Brady's hair.

I saw men halting to look at her
sauntering along, not seeming to care
about those ever ready to stand and stare.

I knew that men, if they knew, would envy me as I
combed that wild, flowing bundle of gold
for her walks in the mesmerised streets of the city.

I went deeper into her hair than anyone.
I knew she was happy, this made me feel good.
Then why am I dumped into roadside mud?

I once heard a would-be lover say, 'Sheila,
let me serve you till the day I die.'
She shook her head. Was it flowing gold made him cry?

Leaver

When I left her, she put her back to the door
and said, 'Time for another glass of wine.
There are many things to celebrate.
To start with, the house is mine.'

Money

I always knew they loved me
        but never thought they could,
given the many problems,
        make me their god.

One problem with my divinity
        is that it favours only a few
who continue to adore me
        while the rest persist, make do.

That's the story down the years
        and will always be.
Then why not rest and ask yourself
        if you understand me?

I respond to such attention,
        I'll show you what to do
until you find your special way
        to join the favoured few

Question and Answer

She turned away from him then
        in the love-steaming bed.
'Where are you going?' he asked.
        'Enough is enough' she said.

Envelope

I arrived in the post this morning
with a couple of others. I was last
to be opened and you were hurt

straightaway. The letter was anonymous
and vicious, even poisonous, and I regret
being the bearer of the scurrilous

language that assaulted you.
I thought you would tear me up
with the letter but you tightened your lips

and left both letter and envelope intact.
I'm still here, containing the judgmental
venom unsigned by the know-all coward.

Hurt and unknowing, you sat there,
wondering who and why. I lay in a drawer.
Stamp me. I'll go anywhere.

I serve love and hate, cowardice and courage
everywhere.

One line only

I am one line only
but according to a witty lady
    I am the most
    impressive line of all:

  'The cheque is in the post.'

Flesh

I crave my kind.
Flesh makes flesh come more alive.
The same is true of minds.

I think, but in a different way.
Here I am, under skin, ready to animate
when you make love or kneel to pray

or work to make a living or play
a game that others love to play or answer
questions when your expression helps your

thought or decide to climb a mountain
or walk a town from one end
to another, talking to a friend

in your mind all the long miles.
I am your joy, your pain, the bearer
of burdens that never go away.

Sometimes I stink. That's no shame.
A wise man said,
I stink, therefore I am.

I help your mind when I can
and it helps me at times. There are
moments when we seem to ignore each other.

As the years go by I feel more pains
but I do my best to go on, go on
through heat and cold and wind and rain

knowing I'm a transient thing
but strangely this is part of my joy,
it makes my ageing self desire to sing

as I see young flesh cross the threshold
of adventure, fit and beautiful,
eager to live days and nights
to their challenging full.

Football

Girls and boys, young men and women
chase me with a vigour
not many know or knew

but nobody on earth
enjoys being kicked around
like I do.

Whisper

When, in a room packed with people,
two lean towards each other's ears
and share,

they often attract more attention
than if they spoke out loud.
Something's going on there, others think

as they witness confidentiality,
the air of secrecy,
the exclusion of all but two.

I think I work best between lovers,
alone in their loving, whispering
what even the walls cannot hear.

I'm like a kind of womb
where moments can be shared
and, in the quietness of minds, remembered.

Gossip and scandal use me a lot.
I never like the way
characters are made to rot

but I have no choice in such matters.
I'm an instrument people use when they wish.
I say the words they want me to say.

Can you hear me?

Loneliness

If you endure me
I will help you
see your friends

in a truer light.
I will give you
challenging memories

of love, language, pain,
faces, what you suffered
and caused others to suffer.

I will help you tolerate time
as, in truth, it is and
is not. I will give a name

to the dark hurt
you have borne for years.
I will help you see and hear

the lies you swallowed,
the lies you told. I am
a kind of savage

education, a teacher without pay,
a traveller who knows your stories
and listens to what you must say

when nobody supports you
and you stand alone
like that man you saw

with his back to a wall
crying in a way that made
passers-by look in

the opposite direction.
That situation
can be the source of your strength,

Endure me, I will make you strong.
Like the bleakest streets and stars
I will make you know you belong

to that silent strength living in you
and in the world of near and far,
guiding street, inspiring star.

An hour

So much has happened in my bit
of time I'd need a century at least
to write it down. I have to go now.
Nice to see you. My successor is here.
Time to vanish. I don't dare give advice
to anyone. I only know that most
of what is said and done is forgotten.
Just as well perhaps.
                            I'm gone.

The Forgotten

I speak for millions
yet I speak for nobody.
We are the nobodies of humanity.

Take the smallest village or
the biggest city, we were there
once, like all others.

We passed away as we are still
passing away. You may wish to know
if we help each other. No.

And yet we are together,
bound by pure oblivion.
One word is all we are. Gone.

To where? you ask. Beyond the reach of thought and song,
of past and future, fact and dream,
every version of right and wrong.

There are poets, playwrights, novelists among us,
sculptors, painters, musicians too,
and scientists who once were new.

Look at those who believed they mattered
more than anyone else in town.
Now they are farther down than down.

We are the space beyond all space.
Nothing. Nobody. That's who and where
we are, are not. Does it take

a poem to give us a voice? Or some
Mozart in the midst of us?
O world, hear the sounds of the forgotten,

the sounds of nothing fading away
behind the backs of the furthest stars.
And yet we once loved, worked, had sisters,

brothers, fathers, mothers, teachers, friends.
The forgotten have their own memories
but will never be remembered.

A child once asked this question: What does it mean
to be fair? No answer came. We have
no right to an answer. What can we believe,

wish for, hope for, dream about? If I could speak
to you I would say, remember us
some freezing winter night before you fall

asleep. If you have a prayer
give it to the freezing air. If not,
just whisper, I forget.

We understand.

Daring

It seems I go where I should not go,
do what I should not do,
not to hurt or harm anyone

but to explore beyonds.
The man who split the atom
dared. See what he found.

I find myself in strange places,
in lonely houses, dreaming heads,
half-way up mountains, warm beds.

I enjoy happening in sport,
in the hearts of young men and women
and old golfers out for fun

but serious as well.
I make possible the blissful
adventure of a first kiss.

I've had a long relationship
with the future, with instinct
and impulse and the dark gambler

who never seems to rest.
He sees challenges in clouds,
craves fresh danger, enters lost

and lonely minds, urges them on
to wide-eyed possibility
and scorn for caution.

When those who risk me
return to what we dub normality
they have images stored in memory

and feel as if they have lived
in ways they never lived before
and perhaps never will again.

See that man sitting on his own,
as usual? He'll talk to you if you wish.
He dared walk across Europe to Russia

alone. He returned strong, with scars.
He speaks with the calm conviction of truth.
We enjoyed each other, and the various wars

that gave him his dignified authority,
his refusal to be vain,
his (dare this pen say love?) of the helplessly human.

Steps

There are ninety-seven of us
which you must quickly climb
if you're to get to that meeting

in time. And what do you do?
You start thinking of the one
hundred and eleven you climbed

some fifty years ago to reach
the top of the old castle where
she waited to kiss you over

and over again though you were out
of breath for a while after arriving
at your dream. Now you're breathing

heavily after a mere twenty but somehow
you keep climbing. She's in your mind
after fifty years and you find

the guts to continue up and up
until, unbelievably, you reach the top
and flop into a seat that some

kind heart placed there at the summit.
Head down, out of breath, you thank the dream.
Where is she? Not for years. You're in time for the meeting.

We are like the future, a challenge
you can face or avoid. We neither help
nor hinder. We're there at the edge

of your determination. Some turn back,
take the long route. Perhaps they're wise.
We relish those who rise

to the challenge though steps may become
mountains. Fifty years. Old man, we think
you deserve a young, rewarding kiss.

Sneeze

Of the many millions who have enjoyed me
over the years, may I mention one
stocky, hard-working gentleman

who made a living baking bread
for the inhabitants of his small town.
Each morning, he scanned the heavens for a sign of sun

and, from his front door, usually found a vital trace.
He offered his face to the sky, closed his eyes,
waited with what seemed the patience of a saint

and then
sneezed
with a gusto that shook the little town

awake. The stocky gentleman stayed
looking at the sky in gratitude
and said to street and cloud

'Thanks be to God
for that happy sneeze.
Now for a full smell
of my well-baked bread.'

Pain

I'm a steady presence now
a kind of company hard enough to bear
but not intolerable.

You can't see me but you know
I'm there. I know the touch
of your fingers.

I remind you of people, of mistakes, lies,
misadventures, of you being blind
to what was happening

within and around you.
I know you better than most people.
I live in you.

I know why you love to laugh
and why you try not to cry.
I have become a kind of adviser

to you. This morning I feel your need
of a few clear words as I go deeper
into your bones.

Get up. Bear me. Face yourself and the world.
Hear the silent cries.
Hello to passing eyes,

many of whom I know quite well.
Most folk around me are local.
I'm universal.

The other way

Some people like to look in my direction,
the other way.
They do so because they cannot think
of anything to say.

At times they do so because they are
telling a lie
and must not look directly in
listening eyes.

I am the almost perfect escape route,
the shrewd alternative,
door, gate, exit sign,
live and let live.

Morally wobbly, perhaps,
or should I say of course?
I know I help some dubious hearts
but I've seen worse.

Still, that does not excuse me
when it comes to lies.
Few things are more challenging
than honest eyes.

Honesty

'Poetry is honesty,' the gruff old saint said
out of a heart that longed for God.
He described me the best he could

but I wonder about poetry.
Poetry may be honesty
but is honesty poetry?

No, though now and then, I may be
but I never hesitate, if necessary,
to show my brutality

to certain hand-shakers, arse-lickers, foxy
versifiers. Do I fit in with style?
Do we get on with each other?

When the most honest man who ever lived
was asked questions few could begin
to answer, he often told a story

and let his listeners make of it what
they would or could. Listeners still do exactly that.
What does anyone know of a story's heart?

I live in stories, stories that are not lies.
I like to walk the street with truth
at my side. I look in truth's eyes.

and see what I wish to be
but rarely achieve. Minds, mouths and
hearts give me a different identity.

What am I, then? I wander in search
of a voice that will speak me as I am,
a voice that believes it knows where I come from

and where I'm going. I may enlighten,
astonish, hurt, accuse, re-kindle lost love,
give birth to hate, change lives of women

and men, but I say what I must say, do
what I must do. I am not ashamed to look
in the eyes of truth, we are friends who

see and say what friendship is. If living
is a search for fair definitions, let me try
to love true eyes, challenge every lie.

The polished hypocrite arrives to scoff.
The grumpy old saint barks, 'Fuck off.'

Favourite word

The day I heard you say I was
your favourite word, I wondered
what is the meaning of meaning

and found no answer. To you
I mean what is beyond my grasp
and if I help you to cope

with those unshareable horrors
you mentioned, I am more happy
than I dare to say.

Going alone through stricken cities,
seeing sickness, poverty, disease
and the slick plague of unawareness,

witnessing post-modern forms of betrayal
thrive where hope seems to have died,
you said you summon me into your head

and you are somehow able to endure
the unendurable. You said I help you
to act where action seemed unthinkable.

I am only a word. One word.
Like all my kind, I live waiting to be used.
Times I feel useless. And then a child,

woman or man brings me into the light
like one of the roses you're looking at now
in a coffee shop in a trafficking town.

It is autumn. The roses are withering.
Another summer gone for good.
I am waiting in your blood.

Fingers

Such a strange range of activities!
We go from loving caresses
to savage strangulation,

from caring for the sick
to hurting the healthy,
from sport to war to tricks

with cards, from lives of theft
to work that helps to keep old people
working. Our urges come from forces

beyond us and our function is to obey.
Obedience is the law we must observe.
We serve, relax, and then again we serve.

Let me speak as one now. Today,
after several years of loving,
she had a wedding ring

placed on her finger. My friends and I
rejoice. May every future caress
deepen her happiness.

She makes me happy too.
I think that fingers serve best
when serving love. May we serve you.

Insider

I belong, I know I belong to a special
place, a special people, a special knowledge
of every other place and people surrounding me.

I was born here, grew up here,
no need for me to travel
to other places. I know them anyway.

I know my neighbours, they know me.
We accept each other, though I am aware
of little poisons now and then.

I know their lives for decades past.
They know mine.
We know when to speak, when to be silent.

This knowledge of silence is the foundation
of tolerant living together
in all seasons, all weathers.

No need, though, to be silent about outsiders,
blow-ins. They simply got it wrong.
They don't belong.

That lost look is no excuse
for being always on the useless verge
or well beyond it.

I've met quite a few. They're all the same.
For them, every house contains strangers.
Every street has no name.

Am I arrogant? Call me that, if you wish.
I say what I know to be true.
I know what it means to belong. Do you?

Smug, I hear you think. No, I'm strong.
Every step I take is on firm ground.
No need to go beyond.

Chain

For years now, I've been around
her neck. My favourite place.
As the years unfold
my friends call me the hangman.
They're sharp, comical, jealous,
made of silver.
I'm made of gold.

Outsider

No matter where I go, I know I'm not there.
I look at those who know they belong.
I live in a place called nowhere.

Sometimes I think my name is difference.
I'm sitting on a bench in Brighton,
walking a dark street in London,

looking at faces in Paris, Washington,
Colorado, Athens, Cork, Manorhamilton.
I'd like to talk to people but they

have their world, I have mine, have I?
Have. World. Possession is the grave
of love, she whispered in my ear

when I was twenty. I never tried again
but embraced the loneliness of freedom.
Work? Yes, I worked. Then I moved on

to see things in a way those who belong
do not. I tend to enjoy what I will
never possess. I sing a different song.

I know there are others who sing it too,
who also live in a place called nowhere.
It's a privilege to see what is beautiful

in worlds that ignore me. Sit there,
see those who will never intrude on my
knowing how a lonely heart is a multitude

with me wherever I go even though
I am not there. Forty years later,
I hear her whisper.

Mercy

I don't know anyone
who doesn't need me
sometime. It's a question

of what they've done
or failed to do.
Yes, I remember the night

you saw the elderly man
being battered in Merrion Square
by three young thugs

and you walked away,
your heart chewing cowardice
to this day.

Failed to do? Done?
Too many to count.
Strange how moments return

from thirty, forty years ago,
moments even now craving
for me as you go

your thinking, guilty way.
All right, name them, ask me
to come to you and I will try

to give you that absolving calm
that helps you to say, guilt aside,
'I am who I am.'

Who am I? I am the fruit
of understanding guilt and admission,
I visit people on the run

from themselves, take them by the hand,
lead them back to where they did
or failed to do whatever it is

robs them of sleep, we talk together
sometimes for several nights
and when I leave that man or woman

a certain peace makes sleep possible.
I am happy I was there.
And by the way, he's still enjoying life,

the elderly man hammered in Merrion Square.

Black

Like all my enemies and friends, I know
I am the best. Forget the widow's ancient garb,
the black dog, the dark, say black, night of the soul,

the blackest night you've ever seen.
Seen? If that night was as black as I
sometimes choose to be, you saw nothing.

When I block things out, they cease to exist.
So some clever soul invented light
in places where I was solitary king.

Did I not trap you once in an
underground Men's loo in New York
when all light failed and I was walls

for you to climb or smash against?
Somehow, you probed and fingered your way
out into a dimly lit corridor

that led upwards to New York light,
always a revelation when you escape
my grip. I rarely get credit

for being light's astute ambassador,
they simply have to banish me
and I blink off when they switch on

the light that proves their eyes are working.
I have such fun with eyes, defining
their limits, enjoying their struggle

to cope with me in a cave or lonely road
where I rule unchallenged for long
winter hours. Sheep, rats, cows, stray dogs

welcome me. But then, the lazy, pale winter sun
shuffles in and sends me into exile
for a sleepy while. Well, that's the style

of dark, say black, and light, say white.
We are what's going on in you, and we
are war and peace. Which is which? See

what you can in light, what you will in me,
what you will in light, what you can in me.
Not everyone sees the ongoing struggle

for mastery. I do. So does light.
Good morning, Jim. Dear Jane, good night.

War

I'm a glutton. For what? For the bodies
of fit young men, for the most part, but
for any bodies, in fact; of children, ladies,

old folk in and out of homes, strollers in streets,
men and women teaching in schools, priests,
people crouched in houses, busy in offices,

bishops, deacons, nuns, anyone aspiring
to anything . I love to feast my eyes
on famous buildings, museums, universities,

skyscrapers, palaces, cathedrals, castles
unbroken by centuries. I am always being
born in the hearts of men intent on winning

something. Quickly I spread disaster,
my delight. Some say 'War is evil',
but there are always those who prefer

to kill and kill. Patriotic stuff.
Heroes full of glory. Bring them home
in bags. Fame.

When will they learn that I delight
in destruction as I hear them prattle
of freedom, democracy, rights?

The Thirty Years War. Nice.
Two World Wars. Nicer still.
Raging on today, tomorrow. I'm always there.

Why? If I knew the answer I wouldn't tell.
A wounded girl weeps for her dead lover,
hero. 'War is evil.' 'War is hell.'

Sometimes, peace breaks out.
I go underground, wait, patient old king.
Soon, I hear the call. Bombs are falling.

There are those who say I can be just.
This time, perhaps?
Put me to the test.

Peace

Here you come, striding up
that leafy street,
looking for me.
I'm here.
Remember sitting under that tree in Pavia?
We were together there
and I knew, for an hour,
your happy blood.
Open your heart now,
let me enter it,
I want to live in you
for good.

www.ingramcontent.com/pod-product-compliance
Lightning Source LLC
Jackson TN
JSHW080854211224
75817JS00002B/34